BYOB8

BYOB8

AN 8-DAY CRASH COURSE ON BUSINESS EDUCATION

DR. YVETTE MAUREEN

Copyright © 2019, 2023 Dr. Yvette Maureen

All rights reserved. No part of this book may be reproduced, stored, or transmitted by any means—whether auditory, graphic, mechanical, or electronic—without written permission of both publisher and author, except in the case of brief excerpts used in critical articles and reviews. Unauthorized reproduction of any part of this work is illegal and is punishable by law.

Because of the dynamic nature of the Internet, any web addresses or links contained in this book may have changed since publication and may no longer be valid. The views expressed in this work are solely those of the author and do not necessarily reflect the views of the publisher, and the publisher hereby disclaims any responsibility for them.

#BYOB8: An 8-Day Crash Course on Business Education

Build Your Own Business 8 (#BYOB8) features 8 essential management and marketing principles that every business leader needs to know before pulling up a chair at the boardroom table.

#BYOB8 is a book for anyone who needs to quickly learn the fundamental concepts of business in eight short days, whether you're the CEO of a startup or a lifelong learner.

#BYOB8 includes customized coursework and quizzes, a glossary of key business terms, and pre-highlighted daily takeaways.

#BYOB8 does 3 things:

1. Helps you create realistic business goals
2. Explains how you can develop and implement the initial steps in fulfilling your business goals
3. Helps you create a strategic business plan

#BYOB8 is a book for anyone who needs to quickly learn the fundamental concepts of business whether you're a CEO of a startup or a lifelong learner.

#BYOB8 frame of mind:

- » **Students:** As you prepare to become a business leader and/or manager, you can utilize **#BYOB8** to further your business acumen. It may be ideal to keep one company in mind while reading this book to help expand your learning and make real-world connections.

- » **Aspiring business leaders:** As you begin your journey to develop your business and lead within your organization, you can utilize the methods and information within **#BYOB8** to develop and grow your business.

- » **Established business leaders:** You can utilize the information presented in **#BYOB8** as a refresher on how to revitalize your business and further your business acumen.

Acknowledgments

Thank you, God!

Publisher
Mynd Matters Publishing

Contents

DAY ONE 1
Planning and Strategic Management

DAY TWO 27
The Marketing Strategy Planning Process and Highlighting Opportunity

DAY THREE 37
Ethics, Corporate Responsibility, and Sustainability

DAY FOUR 45
International Management

DAY FIVE 57
Managing and Performing

DAY SIX 85
Organizational Agility

DAY SEVEN 99
External & Internal Environments: The Competitive Environment

DAY EIGHT 119
External & Internal Environments: The Economic, Legal, Political, Cultural, and Social Environments

DAY ONE

Planning and Strategic Management

"Success is when preparation meets opportunity."

Day One

Planning and Strategic Management

Welcome to Day One!

Think back to a time where you had to plan an event—no matter how large or small! No matter the scale of the event, the preparation tasks have something in common. They require planning and intentional effort to be successful and achieve their purpose. When it comes to understanding what it takes to conceptualize, develop, launch, and sustain a successful business, you can draw from personal experiences and day-to-day life to truly understand how business leaders plan strategically and effectively manage their businesses to dominate their markets and experience success.

The Basic Planning Process

Planning is a decision-making process—you're deciding what to do and how to go about doing it. The important steps to follow during formal planning are like the basic decision-making steps you may take when planning a surprise birthday dinner or community 5K event. In this chapter, we'll describe the basic planning process in more detail along with how managerial decisions and plans fit into the larger purpose of the organization—addressing the firm's strategy, mission, vision, and goals.

Step 1: Situational Analysis

Planning begins with a situational analysis. It may sound more intense than it is! A situational analysis simply refers to the process where you make an assessment of the time and resource constraints that you need to learn, interpret, and summarize. To do a situational analysis well, you should study past events, examine current conditions, and attempt to forecast future trends. In your analysis, remember to consider the internal forces and consistently examine influences from the external environment. The goal of the analysis is the identification and diagnosis of potential issues or problems.

A thorough situational analysis provides information about the decisions you need to make. For example, if you are a manager at a magazine company considering the launch of a sports publication for the teen market, your analysis includes such factors as the number of teens subscribing to magazines, the appeal of the teen market to advertisers, your firm's ability to serve this market effectively, current economic conditions, the level of teen interest in sports, and any sports magazines already serving this market and their current sales. A detailed situational analysis will help you decide whether to proceed with the next step in your magazine launch.

Step 2: Alternative Goals and Plans

After completing the situational analysis, you move on to the planning process. During the planning process, you should use the results of the situational analysis to generate future alternative goals and alternative plans that may be used to achieve those goals. The planning process is where you should unleash your creativity and innovative decision-making! If we continue with our magazine publishing example, the alternatives you might want to consider include whether the magazine should be targeted at young men, young women, or both groups and whether it should be mainly online, through subscriptions, or on newsstands. From this step, you can develop your organizational goals.

Goals are the targets or ends you want to reach. To be effective, goals should have certain qualities, which are easy to remember with the acronym SMART

To be effective, your organizational goals should have certain qualities, which are easy to remember with the acronym SMART:

- » *Specific.* When goals are precise, describing particular behaviors and outcomes, you can more easily determine whether you are actually working toward the goals.

- » *Measurable.* As much as possible, each goal should quantify the desired result so there is no doubt whether it has been achieved.

- » *Attainable (but challenging).* You need to believe that you can reach the goals you are responsible for, or else you may become discouraged. Still, you should feel challenged enough to work hard to achieve the goals.

- » *Relevant.* Each goal should contribute to the organization's overall mission while being consistent with its values, including ethical standards.

- » *Time-bound.* Effective goals specify a target date for completion. Besides knowing what to do, you should know when you need it done by.

An example of a SMART goal for business is:

- » Durning the next quarter, I will increase engagement on my website by 50% by publishing new content three times per week.

Ideally, SMART goals point you in a direction and motivate you to get there. Once you have the goal(s) in mind, then you need to consider how you can make those goals your reality. Plans are the actions or means that a business leader intends to use to achieve goals. At a minimum, planning should outline alternative steps that may lead to the attainment of each goal, name the resources required to reach each goal, and consider the obstacles or barriers that may occur along the way.

Now, let's talk about various types of plans that an organization or even individuals can use as a strategic management strategy. Some plans, called contingency plans, can be referred to as "what if" plans. They include sets of actions that should be taken when initial plans have not worked well or if uncontrollable events in the external environment require a sudden change. Disasters over the years, including natural disasters and global pandemics, have reminded many businesses how important contingency planning can be.

Plans are the actions or means a business leader intends to use to achieve goals.

However, contingency plans are important for more common situations as well. For example, many businesses are affected by increases in gasoline prices, computer breakdowns, changes in consumer tastes, or challenges with human resources. Southwest Airlines initially achieved success as an affordable airline that would "connect people to what's important in their lives" by caring about its customers and employees. However, the airline faced public criticism and embarrassment as the company had to ground 71% of their flights due to a glitch in the scheduling system in the wake of cancellations after a winter storm. The company took days to recover, canceling more than two thousand flights. As a result, most major corporations now have contingency plans in place to respond to a major disaster such as making sure that there is capacity to meet increased needs after a major disruptive event.

Step 3: Goal and Plan Evaluation

After completing the situational analysis and identifying alternative plans and goals, as a business leader, you should take time to evaluate the advantages, disadvantages, and potential effects of each alternative goal and plan. In the goal evaluation process, you should consider how your identified goals align to your business priorities to determine which you will focus on most. During that reflective process, you may decide to eliminate some goals entirely. That's okay! The goal of this process is to refine your goal list. Business leaders should also carefully consider the impact of alternative plans on meeting high-priority goals and pay attention to the cost and the investment return that is likely to result.

For instance, keeping with our magazine publishing example, your evaluation might determine that newsstand sales alone aren't profitable enough to justify the launch. Perhaps you could improve profits with an online edition supplemented by podcasts. To decide, you estimate the costs and expected returns of each alternative.

Step 4: Goal and Plan Selection

Once your goals and plans have been refined, you should evaluate your business priorities and trade-offs. After assessing various goals and plans, you should select the one that is most appropriate and feasible. For example, if your plan is to launch a number of new publications, and you're trying to choose among them, you might weigh the different up-front investments each requires, the size of each market, which one fits best with your existing product line or company image, and so on. Experienced judgment always plays an important role in this process. However, as you will discover, relying on judgment alone may not be the best way to proceed.

> *Relying on judgment alone may not be the best way to proceed.*

A different contingency plan is attached to each scenario. This approach helps you anticipate and manage crises and allows greater flexibility and responsiveness.

Step 5: Implementation

Once you have constructed your goals and plans, it's time to follow the steps you outlined in your plan(s) to achieve your goals. Remember, the best plans are useless if they are not implemented properly. Business leaders must understand the plan, have the resources to implement that plan, and the motivation to carry it out. To create the highest likelihood of a smooth implementation phase, business leaders must be sure to include employees and business members in the previous steps of the planning process. People tend to be more invested in a goal or plan they understand and helped develop.

> *People usually are better informed about and more committed to a goal or plan they helped develop.*

Finally, successful implementation requires the plan to be linked to other systems in the organization, particularly the budget and reward systems. If you do not have a budget or a method to obtain financial resources, the plan is likely doomed. Similarly, goal achievement must be linked to the organization's reward system, which requires using incentive programs to encourage employees to achieve goals and to implement plans properly. Examples of reward systems include commissions, sales, promotions, bonuses, and other rewards based on successful performance.

Step 6: Monitor and Control

Although it is sometimes ignored, the sixth step in the formal planning process—monitoring and controlling—is essential. Without it, you will never know whether your plan is succeeding. As mentioned earlier, planning works in a cycle; it is an ongoing, repetitive process. As a business leader, you must continually monitor the actual performance of your work against your initial goals and plans. You also need to develop control systems to measure performance and take corrective action when plans are implemented improperly or when the situation changes.

Business leaders must continually monitor the actual performance of their work against the initial goals and plans.

S.W.O.T. Analysis and Strategy Formulation

Analyzing the external environment and the internal resources of your organization will provide the information needed to assess its strengths, weaknesses, opportunities, and threats. Such an assessment normally is referred to as the **S.W.O.T. Analysis.** Strengths and weaknesses refer to internal resources. For example, an organization's strengths might include skilled management, positive cash flow, and well-known and highly regarded brands. Weaknesses might be low employee morale and commitment or the absence of reliable partners. Opportunities and threats arise in external and competitive environments. Examples of opportunities are new technologies that allow easier communication with customers or a market niche that is currently underserved. Threats might include the possibility that competitors will enter the underserved niche that is deemed a profitable market.

A S.W.O.T. analysis can help business leaders identify the primary and secondary strategic issues facing an organization. Therefore, the final step is to formulate a strategy that builds on the S.W.O.T. analysis. The strategic goal is to take advantage of available opportunities by 1) capitalizing on the organization's strengths, 2) neutralizing its weaknesses, and 3) countering potential threats.

Extra Attention: Referring back to Step 2, let's plan for your SMART goals. Review the two organizational goals below, then complete one organizational and one personal SMART goal.

Specific	I want to increase our search engine traffic by 10% during the next two months.
Measurable	We will optimize our five best pieces of content to make them even better and aim to secure 10 high-quality backlinks to those pieces of content.
Attainable	If everyone on our team pitches in, this goal is very realistic and attainable.
Relevant	Search engine traffic is the most valuable traffic source for our business. This plan is the best way for us to increase our organic traffic. It directly translates into business success.
Time-Bound	We will accomplish this during the next two months and measure our performance by both our actions and the ensuing results.

Specific	We will respond to all customer questions immediately and resolve issues within 24 hours of receipt.
Measurable	Calls will be answered within three rings of the line. Support tickets will be closed within 24 hours of being opened by a service rep.
Attainable	We will have sufficient service team members on hand to meet the response and resolution metrics.
Relevant	Improving response rates and connecting with customers is the core of our brand; therefore, we must exemplify that quality to all customers.
Time-Bound	Response and resolution metrics will be reviewed every month for compliance. If targets are not achieved, we will implement improvement measures that will restore service levels before the next monthly review.

Specific	
Measurable	
Attainable	
Relevant	
Time-Bound	

Specific	
Measurable	
Attainable	
Relevant	
Time-Bound	

Extra Attention: Let's assess your organization's strengths, weaknesses, opportunities, and threats.

Strengths:
_____
_____
_____

Weaknesses:
_____
_____
_____

Opportunities:
_____
_____
_____

Threats:
_____
_____
_____

Dr. Yvette Maureen

Day One: Planning and Strategic Management

 **Business Builder**

Source: Management: Leading & Collaborating in a Competitive World, By Bateman, T and Snell, S.

EXERCISE 1.1—WHEN BUSINESS STRATEGIES NEED ADJUSTING

Objective

To study why and how a company adjusts its business strategy to adapt to changing external environments.

Instructions

Identify a company that is changing its short and long-term business strategies and answer the following questions. *Hint: You can search online for an article.*

How would you describe the company's former business strategy?

_____

_____

_____

Why is the company changing its strategy? What external forces are encouraging it to change?

___

___

___

How would you describe the new business strategy?

___

___

___

What strategic goals or major targets does the company hope to achieve?

___

___

___

How does the company intend to translate its new strategic goals into operational plans? Which levels of management will carry out these plans?

___

___

___

To what extent do you think the new strategy will be successful in addressing or adapting to the external forces? Explain.

_____

_____

_____

Source: Adapted from R.R. McGrath Jr., Exercises in Management Fundamentals, 1st, p. 15.

EXERCISE 1.2—DISCUSSION QUESTION

Instructions

Think about your answer to the following questions. After reflecting on your response, read the prepared response below. *Hint: You can search online for help with your answer.*

Questions

Question 1: How do strategic, operational, and tactical planning differ?

_____
_____
_____
_____
_____

Question 2: How might the three levels complement one another in an organization?

_____
_____
_____
_____
_____

Answer:

Strategic planning involves making decisions about the long-term goals and strategies for the organization. Strategic plans typically involve an in-depth evaluation of the external environment, normally involve heavy participation on the part of top management and cover a relatively long time frame (from three to five years).

Tactical planning translates the strategic plans into detailed goals and plans that are relevant to a specific part of the organization, often a functional area such as marketing. Tactical plans focus on the major actions required for the unit or division to fulfill its part of the strategic plan. Tactical planning is typically done by middle management with a six-month or one-year focus.

Operational planning identifies the specific procedures and processes required at lower levels of the organization. Operational plans usually cover short periods of time (one to two weeks) and focus on the routine tasks completed by front-line employees as required to support the division in achieving its tactical plans and goals.

It is vitally important that an organization's strategic, tactical, and operational plans are in agreement. If a company's strategic goal is to enter a new market with a new product, it is essential that the tactical plans specify how the product may differ to meet the needs of the new market niche. The operational plans detail methods to reach and serve that market with the new product offering.

EXERCISE 1.4—TEST YOUR KNOWLEDGE

1. To be effective, goals should have open-ended completion times.

    A. True

    B. False

2. In planning, the goal is to come up with a clear and _____ map to follow in future activities.

    A. rigid

    B. flexible

    C. formal

    D. routine

    E. traditional

3. How would a firm's highly regarded brand be listed in a typical SWOT analysis?

    A. As a strength

    B. As a weakness

    C. As an opportunity

    D. As a threat

    E. As a tactic

Answer Key:

1. **(B) FALSE**—To be effective, goals should have certain qualities, which include being specific, measurable, attainable, relevant, and time-bound. (These qualities can be remembered by the acronym SMART.) When goals are precise, describing particular behaviors and outcomes, employees can more easily determine whether they are working toward the goals. Effective goals specify a target date for completion.

2. **(B) FLEXIBLE**—Planning provides individuals and work units with a clear map to follow in their future activities. The map needs to be flexible enough to allow for individual circumstances and changing conditions.

3. **(A) AS A STRENGTH**—An organization's strengths might include skilled management, positive cash flow, and well-known and highly regarded brands.

Day One:
Planning and Strategic Management

 Improve Your Business Vocabulary

Key Marketing Terms

1. **Competitive Rivals:** a firm's closest competitors

2. **Competitor Analysis:** an organized approach for evaluating the strengths and weaknesses of current or potential competitors' marketing strategies

3. **Competitive Environment:** the number and types of competitors the marketing manager must face and how they may behave

4. **Competitor Matrix:** a table depicting the results of a competitor analysis

5. **Economic Environment:** refers to macroeconomic factors including national income, economic growth, and inflation that affect patterns of consumer and business spending

6. **Sustainability:** the idea that it's important to meet present needs without compromising the ability of future generations to meet their own needs.

7. **Sustainable Competitive Advantage:** a marketing mix that customers see as better than a competitor's mix and cannot be quickly or easily copied

8. **Operational Decisions/ Planning:** short-run decisions to help implement strategies

9. **Strategic Planning:** the managerial process of developing and maintaining a match between an organization's resources and its marketing opportunities

Key Management Terms

1. **Barriers to Entry:** conditions that prevent new companies from entering an industry

2. **Competitive Environment:** the immediate environment surrounding a firm; includes suppliers, customers, rivals and the like

3. **Competitive Intelligence:** information that helps managers determine how to compete better

4. **Cooperative Strategies:** strategies used by two or more organizations working together to manage the external environment

5. **Demographics:** measures of various characteristics of the people who make up groups or other social units

6. **Environmental Scanning:** searching for and sorting through information about the environment

7. **Situational Analysis:** a process that planners use (within time and resource constraints) to gather, interpret, and summarize all information relevant to the planning issue under consideration

8. **Strategic Planning:** a set of procedures for making decisions about the organization's long-term goals and strategies

9. **SWOT Analysis:** a comparison of strengths, weaknesses, opportunities, and threats that help executives formulate a strategy

10. **Operational Planning:** the process of identifying the specific procedure and process required at lower levels of the operation

DAY TWO

The Marketing Strategy Planning Process and Highlighting Opportunity

"Know your worth and don't be afraid to quantify it (in salary). If you find that your skills and talents aren't reflected in pay from your company, start building your own"

—Merdochey T. LaFrance
Consultant, Corporate Social Responsibility Specialist,
NonProfit Ideator, Political Strategist

Day Two

The Marketing Strategy Planning Process Highlights Opportunity

In this section, you'll learn how a business strategy requires decisions centered around targeted customers and discover how the marketing mix helps you develop appeals to the target market. Your marketing mix decisions can be organized in terms of the original four Ps—Product, Place, Promotion, and Price. However, the idea isn't just to come up with some final strategy. After all, there are hundreds or even thousands of combinations of marketing mix decisions and target markets strategies that an organization might try. With that In mind, your challenge is to zero in on the best strategy for your organization's goals.

It is useful to think of the marketing strategy planning process as a narrowing down process. You'll start the process with a broad look at a market—paying special attention to customer needs, the businesses objective and resources, and competitors. Using this approach will help you identify new and unique opportunities that might be overlooked if the focus is narrowed too quickly.

There are usually more opportunities and strategic possibilities than a firm can pursue.

In reality, you'll likely have more opportunities and strategic possibilities than you can pursue. Each one will have its own advantages and disadvantages. Trends in the external market environment may make a potential opportunity more or less attractive. These complications can make it difficult to zero in on the best target market and marketing mix. However, developing specific qualitative and quantitative screening criteria can help you define which markets to compete in. You should know that the criteria you select in a specific situation stems from the analysis of the company's objectives and resources.

Developing specific qualitative and quantitative screening criteria can help you define what business and which markets to compete in.

 Extra Attention: Let's examine the market surrounding your business. Then, examine any new opportunities.

Customer Needs:
_____
_____
_____

Organization Objectives:

_____

_____

_____

Organization Resources:

_____

_____

_____

Organization Competitors:

_____

_____

_____

NEW Opportunities:

_____

_____

_____

A useful aid for organizing information from the broader market and developing relevant screening criteria is the S.W.O.T. analysis, which we discussed on *Day One*. You'll recall that the strengths and weaknesses come from assessing the company's resources and capabilities. For example, a local farmer's market might have a great reputation in its community (strength) but have limited financial resources (weakness). Opportunities and threats in the S.W.O.T. analysis can emerge from the examination of customers, competition, and the external market environment. The farmer's market might see an opportunity when a growing number of customers in its community show an interest in eating locally grown fruits and vegetables, while a threat could be a drought that limits local farmers' production. With a S.W.O.T. analysis, you can begin to identify strategies to take advantage of strengths and opportunities while avoiding weaknesses and threats.

In the early stages of your search for opportunities, look for customers with needs that are not being satisfied. Of course, potential customers have unique needs that need to be addressed differently because they represent diverse characteristics. d. However, there are often subgroups (segments) of consumers who are similar and could be satisfied with the same marketing mix. As such, it's up to you to identify and understand these different subgroups—with market segmentation. It's important for you to understand that customers are at the heart of using market segmentation and the process of narrowing down to a specific target market. Because of their importance, *people* are considered to be the fifth P in the marketing mix formula.

Extra Attention: Let's narrow down your potential customer base to a more specific target market.

A marketing mix (product, price, place, promotion, people) won't get you a competitive advantage if it just meets customer needs in the same way as some other firm. You want to identify customers' needs that are not being addressed or that you can do a better job meeting than the competition. Assessing three things—customers, competitors, and the company—helps business leaders identify possible strategies to differentiate their marketing mix

You want to identify customers' needs that are not being addressed or might be met better than the competition.

from the competition. **Differentiation** is what occurs when you ensure that the marketing mix is distinct from what is available from a competitor.

Sometimes differences are based mainly on one important element of the marketing mix—say, an improved product or faster delivery. However, differentiation will often require that your business fine-tunes all the elements of its marketing mix to the specific needs of a distinctive target market. Target customers are more likely to recognize your firm as "different" when it is viewed as uniquely meeting their needs.

Sometimes differences are based mainly on one important element of the marketing mix—say, an improved product or faster delivery.

For example, in Northern Europe, many auto buyers are particularly concerned about driving safely on snowy roads. So, Audi offers a permanent four-wheel-drive system called Quattro that helps the car to hold the road. Audi's advertising emphasizes this point of differentiation. Rather than displaying the car, ads feature things that are very sticky (like bubblegum)! And the only text is the headline "sticks like Quattro" along with the Audi brand name. While Audi's have other strengths, its target market appreciates how a car handles in the snow. So, when these customers look to buy a new car, they will likely consider an Audi.

Day Two:
The Marketing Strategy Planning Process Highlights Opportunity

 Improve Your Business Vocabulary

Key Marketing Terms

1. **Competitive Advantage:** a firm has a marketing mix that the target market sees as better than a competitor's mix

2. **Differentiation:** the marketing mix is distinct from and better than what's available from a competitor

3. **Implementation:** putting marketing plans into operation

4. **Market Development:** trying to increase sales by selling present products in new markets

5. **Market Penetration:** trying to increase sales of a firm's present products in its present markets—probably through a more aggressive marketing mix

6. **Marketing Mix:** the controllable variables that the company puts together to satisfy a target group

7. **Marketing Plan:** a written statement of a marketing strategy and the time-related details for carrying out the strategy

8. **Marketing Program:** blends all of the firm's marketing plans into one big plan

9. **Marketing Strategy:** specifies a target market and a related marketing mix

10. **Mass Marketing:** the typical production-oriented approach that vaguely aims at everyone with the same marketing mix

11. **Product Development:** offering new or improved products for present markets

12. **Target Marketing:** a marketing mix is tailored to fit some specific target customers

Key Management Terms

1. **Business Strategy:** the major actions by which a business competes in a particular industry or market

2. **Differentiation Strategy:** a strategy an organization uses to build competitive advantage by being unique in its industry or market segment along one or more dimensions

3. **Strategic Management:** a process that involves managers from all parts of the organization in the formulation and the implementation of strategic goals and strategies

DAY THREE

Ethics, Corporate Responsibility, and Sustainability

Start a business based on a consumer-focused need that you can solve. Have a tight market focus initially. And then begin to think beyond your base consumer.

—Javonte Anyabwele, Global Business Executive, Fortune 200 Company

Day Three

Ethics, Corporate Responsibility, and Sustainability

Extra Attention: Recall the last time you were faced with an ethical dilemma in the workplace. Describe your approach, the expected outcome, and the actual outcome.

_____

_____

_____

_____

_____

_____

_____

Ethical Decision Making

Making an ethical decision is not always easy and takes a considerable amount of knowledge and time. For individuals, ethical decisions are often made based on prior knowledge and social influences. This is often the same for many of the organizations you are familiar with like Honest Tea, Proctor & Gamble, and Exxon. As a business leader, making ethical decisions can be a daunting task because you have to consider that the choices you make will potentially affect the livelihoods of hundreds of employees and thousands of customers. When making these decisions, you may face pressures that are difficult to resist. Keep in mind that it's not always clear that a problem has ethical dimensions; they don't hold up signs that say "Hey, I'm an ethical issue, so think about me in moral terms!" Making ethical decisions takes moral awareness (realizing the issue has ethical implications), moral judgment (knowing what actions are morally defensible), and moral character (the strength and persistence to act in accordance with your ethics despite the challenges).

> ***Making ethical decisions takes moral awareness (realizing the issue has ethical implications), moral judgment (knowing what actions are morally defensible), and moral character (the strength and persistence to act in accordance with your ethics despite the challenges).***

Social Responsibility as an Ethical Dimension

Economic and legal responsibilities are the most basic aspects of social responsibility. Beyond these dimensions lie marketing ethics—principles and standards that define acceptable conduct in marketing as determined by various stakeholders, including the public, government regulators, private-interest groups, consumers, industries, and the organization itself. The basis of these principles has been codified as law and regulations to encourage marketers to conform to society's expectations of conduct. For instance, Russia's invasion of Ukraine ushered in a new era of cyberwarfare and exacerbated the already-precarious threat landscape. In addition, there was a spate of new privacy and cyber laws and regulations due in large part to new technologies and the increased attention on protective privacy and cyber hygiene. There was also a substantial uptick in regulatory scrutiny and enforcement, as well as civil and criminal litigation, which further amplified the focus and urgency of privacy and cybersecurity issues. Although the full impact of these developments is yet to be realized, one thing is clear: the challenges and opportunities are extraordinary, far reaching, and unprecedented. The breach at Target that led to the theft of 40 million credit and debit card accounts led to lawsuits and heavy reputational damage to the firm. Society expects companies to be alert in guarding their personal information, and Target clearly ignored red flags that would have enabled it to stop the theft. Target CEO Gregg Steinhafel resigned because of the fallout.

However, marketing ethics goes beyond legal issues. Ethical marketing decisions foster trust, which helps to build long-term marketing relationships with your customers. Studies have shown that transparency about how products are produced, as well as how a firm's philanthropic activities give back to the community, creates trust and intentions to purchase. This also creates positive word-of-mouth communication about the firm. As a business leader, you should be aware of the ethical standards of acceptable conduct from several viewpoints—the company, industry, government, customers, special-interest groups, and society at large. When marketing activities deviate from accepted standards, there can be a breakdown resulting in customer dissatisfaction, lack of trust, and lawsuits. When you engage in activities that deviate from accepted principles, it becomes difficult (if not impossible) to continue some business exchanges. The best time to deal with such problems is during the strategic planning process, not after major problems materialize.

An **ethical issue** is an identifiable problem, situation, or opportunity requiring an individual or organization to choose from among several actions that must be evaluated as right or wrong, ethical or unethical. Anytime an activity causes business leaders or customers in their target market to feel manipulated or cheated, an ethical issue exists, regardless of the legality of that activity. For example, the FDA has asked drug and meat companies to stop giving antibiotics to livestock as a means of speeding up their growth. However, before the

> *Anytime an activity causes business leaders or customers in their target market to feel manipulated or cheated, an ethical issue exists.*

FDA got involved, Perdue Farms had already required its farmers to end the practice due to concerns from customers. Market concerns over the safety of food turned this practice into an ethical issue. As a result of customer pressure, companies such as Perdue, Tyson, and Walmart began selling meat products without antibiotics even before the issue caught regulators' attention. There's also no pork or beef giant that's taken the antibiotic-free leap like Perdue did for chicken. That could change in the years ahead: McDonald's, the world's largest beef purchaser, announced at the end of 2022 that it plans to reduce antibiotic use in its beef supply chain. However, the announcement didn't come with a timeline, which worries advocates like Wellington, and the company has failed to make good on other pledges.

Business Ethics

Insider trading, sweatshops and modern slavery, bribery and kickbacks, famous court cases, and other scandals have created a perception that business leaders use illegal means to gain a competitive advantage, increase profits, or improve their personal positions. It becomes problematic when neither young managers nor consumers believe top executives are doing a good job of establishing high ethical standards. Unfortunately, some even joke that the term *business ethics* is a contradiction in itself. You, as a business leader, have an obligation to conduct your business in a way that aligns with the ethical standards of your industry.

Day Three:
Ethics, Corporate Responsibility, and Sustainability

 Improve Your Business Vocabulary

Key Management Terms

1. **Business Ethics:** the moral principle and standards that guide behavior in the world of business

2. **Ethical Issue:** a situation, problem, or opportunity in which an individual must choose among several actions that must be evaluated as morally right or wrong

3. **Ethical Responsibility:** meeting other social expectations not written as law

4. **Ethics:** the system of rules that governs the ordering of values

DAY FOUR
International Management

"There are plenty of hard-working people who are not very successful because doing hard work is only a single ingredient to success and not the entire recipe."

—Chris "Fish" Fisher, Founder & Business Coach, Mahogany Moguls

Day Four

International Management

Entering International Markets

If you're an International business leader, you must decide on the best means of entering an overseas market when considering expanding your business globally. The five basic ways to expand overseas are exporting, licensing, entering into a joint venture, and setting up a wholly owned subsidiary in the host country.

As a rule, the approaches that are strategic around handling greater risk and require a large upfront investment offer the best benefit of greater control over the marketing mix used.

These strategic decisions apply whether your business is just focused on its domestic market or is also trying to reach target customers in international markets. However, business leaders typically face differences in international markets that require additional choices. In the external market environment, culture and laws are almost always different and political environments involve more risk. As such, we'll briefly discuss five basic ways to enter international markets. As a rule, the approaches that are strategic around handling greater risk and require a large upfront investment offer the best benefit of greater control over the marketing mix used.

> **Extra Attention:** What do you believe are the advantages and disadvantages of global expansion?

_____

_____

_____

_____

_____

_____

Exporting

Most manufacturing companies begin global expansion as exporters and later switch to one of the other modes (discussed below) for serving an overseas market. The main advantage of exporting is that it provides scale economies (cost advantages where fixed costs are spread out over an increase in volume produced/ sold). However, exporting has a number of drawbacks. First, exporting from a company's home base may be inappropriate if low-cost, high-skill labor is available in the domestic location. A second drawback of exporting is that high transportation costs can make it costly, particularly in the case of bulk products. A third drawback is that host countries can impose (or threaten to impose) tariff barriers. Trade arrangements, including the World Trade Organization, NAFTA, and APEC, work to minimize this risk. However, tariffs continue to affect trade between countries in various industries.

Companies begin to market internationally by selling what the firm already produces to foreign markets. You may choose to start exporting just to get rid of surplus inventory. If you do that, you may decide to change very little (if anything) about the products, the label, or even the instructions when exporting and may struggle in the international market. However, other businesses may choose to move beyond that and work closely with intermediaries to develop appropriate marketing mix changes. Business leaders in the latter group tend to be more successful and can adjust to customer preferences while managing import and export taxes, shipping, exchange rates, and actively recruit (or work with) wholesalers and retailers in the foreign country.

Licensing

Licensing means selling the right to use some process, trademark, patent, or another right for a fee or royalty. If good business partners are available, this can be an effective way for a domestic firm to enter a new market as a licensor. The licensee (buyer) in the foreign market takes most of the risk because it makes an initial investment to get started. The licensee in the foreign market also does most of the marketing strategy planning for the markets it is licensed to serve.

Management contracting means that the seller (the licensor) provides only management and marketing skills while others own the production and distributing facilities. Some mining and oil refineries operate this way—and Hilton operates hotels all over the world with local owners using this method. This is another relatively low-risk approach to international marketing.

In sum, international licensing is an arrangement by which a licensee in another country buys the rights to manufacture a company's product in its own country for a negotiated fee (typically royalty payments on the number of units sold). The licensee then puts up most of the capital necessary to get the overseas operation going. The advantage of licensing is that the company need not bear the cost and risks of opening up an overseas market. However, a problem arises when a company licenses its technological expertise to overseas companies.

Sports licensing agreements help promote teams or individual athletes through merchandise. Such contracts give licensing companies the right to use a team's name and logos. Sports licensing is beneficial for both parties. For businesses, it is an opportunity to reach a particular market and for the sports organization, it is a way of advertising their name. However, certain challenges are common to the industry. One of the major issues that the sports licensing field faces is counterfeiting, and fraudulent activity associated with merchandise. It is difficult to avoid this problem even when the trademark is registered through the licensing agreement. Noticing and attempting to stop all counterfeit items from being manufactured and sold under a licensed trademark is a complicated task. However, it is possible to reduce the number of such products by placing more responsibility on the licensor. The licensor should manage the process and quality of the items manufactured by the licensee. Therefore, to decrease the number of cases of fraudulent merchandise, teams and sports organizations should carefully control the work done by the manufacturer.

Joint Ventures

In a **joint venture,** your domestic business would enter into a partnership with a foreign firm. As with any partnership, operating policy decisions must be made regarding how much profit is desired and how fast it should be paid out. This approach can be very attractive to both parties where a close working relationship can be developed—perhaps based on one business's technical and marketing know-how and a foreign partner's knowledge of the market and political connection. Typically, both parties must make significant investments and agree on the marketing strategy. Once a joint venture is formed, it can be difficult to end it if things aren't working out.

Establishing a joint venture with a company in another country has been a popular means of entering a new market. Joint ventures benefit a company through (1) the local partner's knowledge of the host country's competitive conditions, culture, language, political systems, and business systems and (2) the sharing of development costs and/or risks with the local partner.

However, joint ventures have their problems even though they sound like a perfect solution to expanding. First, as in the case of licensing, a company runs the risk of losing control over its technology to its venture partner. Second, companies may find themselves at odds with one another. For example, one joint venture partner may want to move production to a country where demand is growing, but the other would prefer to keep its factories at home running at full capacity. Conflict over who controls what within a joint venture is a primary reason many fail. To offset these disadvantages, experienced business leaders strive to iron out technology, control, and other potential conflicts up front, when they first negotiate the joint venture agreement.

Direct Investments

When a foreign market looks really promising, a firm may want to take a bigger step with a direct investment. **Direct Investment** means that a parent firm has a division (or owns a separate subsidiary firm) in a foreign market. This gives the parent company firm control of business strategy planning.

Direct investment requires a big commitment and usually entails greater risk. For example, if a local market has economic or political problems, the firm cannot easily leave. Still, there are benefits. With direct investment, the firm does not have to share profits with a partner. In addition direct investment:

- » Helps the local job market by providing jobs
- » Allows a company to build a strong presence in a new market
- » Helps the firm develop a good reputation with the government and customers in the host country
- » Helps a firm learn more about a new market

Extra Attention: Now that you have studied the risks and rewards of the traditional ways to expand overseas, how has your consideration of global expansion changed?

_____

_____

_____

_____

_____

Day Four: International Management

 Business Builder

Source: Management: Leading & Collaborating in a Competitive World, By Bateman, T and Snell, S.

 EXERCISE 4.1—DISCUSSION QUESTIONS

Instructions

Consider your answer to the following questions. After reflecting on your responses, read the prepared response below. *Hint: You can search online for help with your answer.*

Questions

Why have franchises been so popular as a method of international expansion in the fast-food industry? Contrast this with high tech manufacturing where joint ventures and partnerships have been more popular. What accounts for the differences across industries?

_____

_____

_____

_____

Answer:

The key to the fast food industry is visibility and that means locations. The franchiser has to be able to promote the product using mass media and this requires as many locations as possible offering identical products. Franchising is the optimal approach because it allows for rapid expansion in terms of the number of locations (since the franchisee provides much of the financing). The franchise agreement requires that the franchisee operates in a specific manner although maintaining quality control is not always easy.

By contrast, a high tech manufacturing firm is looking for a limited number of locations where the emphasis can be placed on quality production. While the manufacturer is highly skilled in the production end of the business, it is often not as familiar with the host country's competitive conditions, culture, political system, etc., and thus needs a professional and knowledgeable local partner.

In the case of franchising, the cost associated with one or two franchises failing is not particularly high. They can be readily replaced. However, the risk associated with establishing a high tech manufacturing operation is much greater, and thus the manufacturer is usually looking for both hands-on control and a long-term relationship, and a partnership or joint venture better provides for this need.

Day Four: International Management

 Improve Your Business Vocabulary

Key Marketing Terms

1. **Channel of Distribution:** any series of firms or individuals who participate in the flow of products from producer to final user or consumer

2. **Contractual Channel Systems:** various channel members agree by contract to cooperate with each other

3. **Exporting:** selling some of what the firm produces to foreign markets

4. **Licensing:** selling the right to use some processes, trademark, patent, or another right for a fee or royalty

5. **International Marketing:** developing and performing marketing activities across national boundaries

6. **Joint Venture:** in international marketing, a domestic firm entering into a partnership with a foreign firm

7. **Vertical Integration:** acquiring firms at different levels of channel activity

8. **Multichannel Distribution:** when a producer uses several competing channels to reach the same target market; perhaps using several intermediaries in addition to selling directly

DAY FIVE
Managing and Performing

"Do not be surprised by people's lack of support. Their reasons are unknown and should not be taken personally. Instead, refocus your thoughts and appreciate your supporters. Pray harder, work smarter, and let your success speak for itself."

—Brandon Okpalobi
CEO, DIBIA Athletic Development
Founder, DIBIA Dream
President, Siyanse

Day Five

Managing and Performing

Managing for a Competitive Advantage

Organizations have to gain and sustain advantages over competitors to survive and win over time. Firms gain competitive advantages by being better than their competitors at doing valuable things for customers. But what does this mean, specifically? To succeed, you, as a business leader, must deliver on performance. The fundamental success drivers of performance are innovation, quality, service, speed, cost competitiveness, and sustainability.

Firms gain competitive advantages by being better than the competitors at doing valuable things for customers.

Innovation

You must continually innovate. Innovation is the introduction of new goods and services. Your firm must adapt to changes in consumer demands and to new competitors. Products don't sell forever; in fact, all around us, new products replace old products. Your firm must innovate, or it will die. Likewise, you have to be ready with new ways to communicate with customers and deliver the products to them. The Internet allows merchants to bypass traditional distribution channels and reach buyers directly; therefore, traditional business leaders had to learn how to innovate to remain competitive.

The fundamental success drivers of performance are innovation, quality, service, speed, cost competitiveness, and sustainability.

The need for innovation is partly driven by globalization (which we discussed on *Day Four*). One obvious reason for that is that facilities in other countries, for example, can manufacture appliances or write software code at a lower cost than facilities in the United States. U.S. facilities thus operate at a disadvantage and must provide something their foreign competitors can't. That often requires delivering something new.

Your firm must innovate, or it will die.

Innovation is today's Holy Grail!

Innovation is today's Holy Grail! Like the other sources of competitive advantages, innovation comes from people. It must be a strategic goal, and you must be able to manage it properly.

Innovation and Market Changes Create Opportunities

Successful new products are critical in driving profitable growth for new and established companies. iRobot pioneered a fast-growing new product market—computer-controlled cleaning tools. You might be familiar with the Roomba. It meets customer needs in new ways, similar to how the iPod, iPhone, and other innovations in digital media changed personal entertainment. In fact, constant reminders of how old products are replaced with new products are all around us. Digital recorders have made VCRs for TVs obsolete. Likewise, cell phones have replaced landline phones and point-and-shoot cameras. Developing new product ideas is critical for businesses because they disrupt old ways of doing things.

These innovations show that products, customer behavior, and competition change rapidly over time. These changes create opportunities and pose challenges as well.

Next, let's take a look at how successful new products are developed and what you need to know and do to successfully manage product growth. We'll start by explaining the cycle of growth and decline that new product innovations go through. When you understand the stages in this cycle, you'll see why it is so critical for a firm to have an effective new-product development process—and why the challenges of managing a product change as the product matures.

Dr. Yvette Maureen

Managing Products over Their Life Cycles

Revolutionary products create new product markets. Competitors are always developing and copying new ideas and products—making existing products out of date more quickly than ever before. Products, like consumers, go through life cycles. To remain competitive, organizations must combine innovation and knowledge of product lifecycles with market knowledge.

The **product life cycle** describes the stages new product idea goes through from beginning to end. The product life cycle is divided into four major stages: (1) market introduction, (2) market growth, (3) market maturity, and (4) sales decline. The product lifecycle concerns new types (or categories) of products in the market, not just what happens to an individual brand.

You'll likely need to change your marketing mix during a product's life cycle. The nature of competition changes, and customer's attitudes and needs may change over the product life cycle. As a result, the product may be aimed at entirely different target markets at different stages of its life cycle. Further, total sales of the product—by all competitors in the industry—vary in each of the four stages. Sales move from very low in the market introduction stage to high at market maturity and then back to low in the sale decline stage. More importantly, the profit picture changes too.

The Product Life Cycle

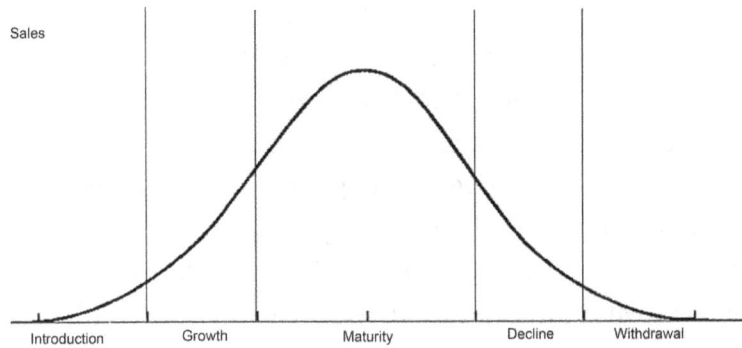

In the **market introduction** stage, sales are low as a new idea is first introduced. Even if the product offers superior value, customers don't know about it because they aren't looking for it. Informative promotion is needed to tell potential customers about the advantages and use of the new-product concept. Even though a firm promotes its new product, it takes time for customers to learn that it is available. Most companies experience loss during the introduction stage because they spend so much money on product, place, and promotion development.

> *Even though a firm promotes its new product, it takes time for customers to learn that the product is available.*

In the **market growth** stage, industry sales grow fast, but industry profits rise and start falling. The innovator begins to make big profits as more and more customers buy. Soon competitors see the opportunity and enter the market. After East African Breweries created a sensation in Nigeria with its nonalcoholic malt beverage Alvaro,

Coca-Cola followed eight months later with its malt drink Noida. This example shows that some just copy the most successful product. Still, others try to improve it to compete better or refine their offering to appeal to target markets.

Market growth can be the moment when a business reaps its biggest profits. The market growth stage is typically a time of rapid sales and earnings growth for companies with effective strategies. However, towards the end of this stage, industry profits begin to decline as competition increases and customers become more sensitive to price.

The **market maturity** stage occurs when industry sales level off and competition gets more challenging. At this stage, many aggressive competitors have entered the race for profits. Industry profits drop because promotion costs rise, and some competitors cut prices to attract more sales. There is a downward pressure on prices. Less efficient firms cannot compete with this pressure—and they drop out of the market.

New firms may still enter the market at this stage, increasing the competition even more! Customers who are happy with their current relationship won't switch to a new brand. So, late entrants usually have a tough battle. Persuasive promotion becomes essential during the market maturity stage because products may differ only slightly between companies.

In the United States, the markets for most cars, most household appliances, and consumer packaged goods like breakfast cereal, carbonated

> ***Persuasive promotion becomes important during the market maturity stage because products may differ only slightly.***

soft drinks, and laundry detergents are in market maturity. This stage may continue for many years until a new product idea comes along—even though individual brands or models come and go.

During the **sales decline** stage, new products replace the old. Price competition from dying products grows intense, but firms with strong brands may make profits until the end because they have successfully differentiated their products. Reminder promotion may be a marketing strategy during the decline stage of the product lifecycle.

> *Reminder promotion may be a marketing strategy during the decline stage of the product lifecycle.*

As new products go through their introduction stage, the old products maintain sales momentum by appealing to their most loyal customers or those who are slow to try new ideas. These conservative buyers might switch later—smoothing the sales decline of the old product.

A firm may introduce or drop a specific product during any stage of the product lifecycle. For example, a copycat brand introduced during the market growth stage may never get sales at all and suffer a fast decline before ever getting off the ground. For example, Walmart tried to rent DVDs by mail after Netflix was already established as the market leader. When customers did not see Walmart's marketing mix as better, it failed to attract enough customers and closed operations.

A product idea can also be in a

> *A product idea can also be in a different life-cycle stage in different markets.*

different life cycle stage in different markets. For example, milk is in the market maturity stage in the United States. U.S. consumers drink 18 times more milk than Asian consumers—where milk is in the market introduction stage. Some firms in the dairy business are trying to grow the Asian market. To appeal to the Asian palate, they are selling milk with added flavors like ginger and honey. As such, strategy planners who naïvely expect sales of an individual product to follow the general product lifecycle pattern are likely to be surprised.

Quality

In general, quality is the excellence of your product. The importance of quality and the standards for acceptable quality have increased dramatically in recent years. Customers now demand high-quality goods and services, often accepting nothing less.

Customers now demand high-quality goods and services, and often they will accept nothing less.

Historically, quality pertained primarily to physical goods that customers bought, and it referred to attractiveness, lack of defects, reliability, and long-term dependability. The traditional approach to quality was to check work after it was completed and then eliminate defects, using inspection and statistical data to determine whether products were up to standards. That was standard operating procedure until W. Edwards Deming, J.M. Juran, and other quality gurus convinced managers to take a complete approach to achieving total quality management

(TQM); Don't worry, we'll discuss this in detail later! TQM includes preventing defects before they occur, achieving zero defects in manufacturing, and designing products for quality. The goal is to solve and eradicate all quality-related problems from the beginning and live a philosophy of continuous improvement in how the company operates.

> **The goal is to solve and eradicate from the beginning all quality-related problems and to live a philosophy of continuous improvement.**

Providing world-class quality requires a thorough understanding of what quality is. Quality can be measured by product performance, customer service, reliability (avoidance of failure or breakdown), conformance to standards, durability, and aesthetics. When you identify specific quality requirements, you can identify problems, target needs, set performance standards more precisely, and deliver world-class value.

Service

It's important for you to understand that quality isn't just about the product itself; it's also about the services that customers receive. This dimension of quality is particularly important because the service sector has come to dominate the economy. Services include intangible products such as insurance, hotel accommodations, medical care, and haircuts.

> **Service means giving customers what they want or need when they want it.**

Service means giving customers what they want or need when they want it. It is focused on continually meeting the customers' needs to establish mutually beneficial long-term relationships. For instance, in addition to providing the actual programs, software companies may help their customers identify requirements, set up computer systems, and perform maintenance. An important dimension of service quality is making it easy and enjoyable for customers to experience a service or to buy and use products.

It can be challenging to provide consistent service quality. People are just not as consistent in their actions as machines or computers. In addition, service quality often depends on a service provider interpreting each customer's needs. For example, a hairstylist must ask good questions and interpret a customer's response before providing the right cut. As a result, a person doing a specific service job may perform one specific task correctly but fail the customer in many other ways. Two keys to improving service quality are (1) training and (2) empowerment.

Every employee who interacts with customers should be trained on customer service and engagement. Many firms require a minimum of 40 hours a year of training. Good training usually includes roleplaying customer requests and problems. A rental car attendant who is rude or inattentive when a customer is trying to return a car may leave the customer dissatisfied—even if the rental car was perfect.

All employees in contact with customers need training.

You likely won't be able to afford an army of managers to inspect how each employee implements a strategy.

> **Empowerment means giving employees the authority to correct a problem without first checking with management.**

Quality cannot be "inspected." It must come from the people who do the service jobs. So, firms that commit to service quality empower employees to determine the best ways to satisfy customer needs. Empowerment means giving employees the authority to correct a problem without first checking with management. At the Ritz Carlton, for instance, an empowered room-service employee knows it's OK to run across the street to buy the specific brand of bottled water a guest requests.

To deliver high-quality goods and services that satisfy customer needs, managers must show that they are committed to doing things right to satisfy customers and that quality is everyone's job. Without top-level support, some people won't get beyond their "business-as-usual" attitude.

Speed

Speed—rapid execution, response, and delivery—often separates the winners from the losers. How fast can you develop and get a new product to market? How quickly can you respond to customer requests? You are far better off if you are faster than the competition and if you can respond quickly to your competitors' actions.

> *You are far better off if you are faster than the competition and if you can respond quickly to your competitors' actions.*

> **You can't get sloppy in your quest to be first. But other things being equal, faster companies are more likely to be the winners, slow ones the losers.**

Speed isn't everything. Don't be sloppy in your quest to be first. But other things being equal, faster companies are more likely to be the winners, slow ones the losers. Even pre-Internet, companies were getting products to market and into the customers' hands faster. Now the speed requirement has increased exponentially. Everything, it seems, has to be done faster than ever.

Speed is no longer just a goal of some companies; it is strategically imperative. In the auto industry, for example, getting faster is essential to keep up with the competition.

Cost Competitiveness

Walmart's efforts are aimed at cost competitiveness, which means (1) pricing its products (goods or services) at levels that are attractive to consumers, and (2) keeping costs low enough so that the company can realize profits. If you can offer a desirable product at a lower price, it is more likely to sell.

One reason that every company must worry about cost is that consumers can easily compare online prices from thousands of competitors. Consumers looking to buy popular items can research the best deals

> **If you can't cut costs and offer attractive prices, you can't compete.**

online. If you can't cut costs and offer attractive prices, you can't compete.

While the cost of poor quality is a loss of customers, the quality efforts we've been discussing can also increase costs. It's easy to fall into the trap of running up unnecessary costs trying to improve some facet of quality that isn't that important to customer satisfaction or retention. Customers may still be satisfied when that happens, but you can't make a profit because of the higher cost. In other words, there isn't a financial return on the money spent to improve quality. A manager should focus on quality efforts that provide the customer with superior value. Focus on quality that doesn't cost more than customers will ultimately be willing to pay.

Focus on quality that doesn't cost more to provide than customers will ultimately be willing to pay.

Sustainability

Avoiding wasteful use of energy can bolster a company's financial performance while also being kind to the environment. Efforts to cut energy waste are just one way to achieve an important competitive advantage. Sustainability is the effort to minimize the use and loss of resources, especially those that pollute the environment or are nonrenewable.

Sustainability is the effort to minimize the use and loss of resources, especially those that are polluting and nonrenewable.

In recent years, corporate efforts aimed at sustainability have fluctuated a bit as environmental laws have been strengthened or loosened. Overall, the worldwide trend has been in the direction of greater concern for sustainability. The clash between rising demand for resources, limited supplies, and changing social attitudes toward environmental protection means that there is likely to be a greater focus on resource productivity, clean-tech industries, and regulations.

Sustainability is about protecting our options. If you do this well, sustainability will allow people to live and work in ways that can be maintained over the long term (generations) without depleting or harming our environmental, social, and economic resources. As many company leaders have discovered, addressing that concern often produces bottom-line benefits. Companies with strong sustainability performance have also become financial winners, including athletic shoe maker Adidas.

Day Five: Managing and Performing

 Business Builder

Source: Management: Leading & Collaborating in a Competitive World, By Bateman, T and Snell, S.

 EXERCISE 5.1—DISCUSSION QUESTION

Instructions

Consider the importance of sustainability. Think about your answer to the following question. After reflecting on your response, read the prepared response below. *Hint: You can search online for help with your answer.*

Question

Can you envision a world that doesn't produce waste? If so, what changes would need to be made before that could happen?

_____

_____

_____

_____

_____

_____

Dr. Yvette Maureen

Answer:

A lot of new procedures would need to be put into place. Converting waste to another product would move the world closer to this concept of no longer producing waste. Countries would need to invest in such a conversion infrastructure. These investments would be slightly offset by the savings in waste management, but such expenditures would be quite costly and not all nations may follow such a "green" route.

EXERCISE 5.2—ARE YOU AN EFFECTIVE MANAGER?

Objective

To examine behaviors of an effective manager

Instructions

Identify 5 additional behaviors that you might observe in an effective manager.

1. Fully supports and carries out company policies
2. Is honest in all matters pertaining to company property or funds
3. Communicates and interprets policy so that it is understood by the members of the organization
4. Seeks means of improving management capabilities and competence
5. Assigns subordinates to the jobs for which they are best suited
6. Makes prompt and clear decisions
7. Encourages associates to submit ideas and plans
8. Stimulates subordinates by means of competition among employees.
9. Is neat in appearance.
10. Participates in community activities as opportunities arise.

11. _____

12. _____

13. _____

14. _____

15. _____

EXERCISE 5.3

Objectives

1. To recognize what behaviors contribute to being a successful manager.

2. To develop a ranking of critical behaviors that you personally believe are important for becoming an effective manager.

Instructions

Part I. Following is a partial list of behaviors in which managers may engage. Rank these items according to their importance for effective management. Put a 1 next to the item that you think is most important, 2 for the next most important, down to 10 for the least important.

Part II. After completing the worksheet, review your list and rank yourself on these same behaviors that might lead to success or greater management effectiveness.

Source: Adapted from Lawrence R. Jauch, Arthur G. Bedeian, Sally A. Coltrin, and William F. Glueck, The Managerial Experience: Cases, Exercises, and Readings, 5th ed. © 1989 South-Western, a part of Cengage Learning, Inc.

Dr. Yvette Maureen

MANAGERIAL BEHAVIORS WORKSHEET

Rank the importance of the managerial behaviors below in order of importance from 1-10. Then, rank yourself on these same qualities on a scale of 1-10.

____ / ____ Collaborates with people from different parts of the organization.

____ / ____ Looks for ways to incorporate technology.

____ / ____ Ensures that services/products are of high quality and delivered on time.

____ / ____ Keeps costs down and looks for ways to be more efficient.

____ / ____ Makes decisions to help achieve the goals of the organization.

____ / ____ Is organized and efficiently allocates resources.

____ / ____ Motivates others to perform at a high level.

____ / ____ Makes sure goals are met and implements changes when necessary.

____ / ____ Exhibits good interpersonal and communication skills.

____ / ____ Is skilled at identifying and resolving problems.

EXERCISE 5.4—TEST YOUR KNOWLEDGE

1. Blake has a coffee shop in Washington, D.C. One thing that attracts busy people to her shop is that she has perfected a way to make lattes and cappuccinos in half the time her competitors take. Which fundamental driver of success has Blake emphasized?

   A. Knowledge

   B. Quality

   C. Cost Competitiveness

   D. Speed

   E. Sustainability

2. Which of the following involves keeping costs low enough so that a company can realize profits while pricing its products at levels that are attractive to consumers?

   A. Total quality

   B. Cost competitiveness

   C. Sustainability

   D. Innovation

   E. Efficiency

3. Which of the following fundamental success drivers of performance has Corey achieved by ensuring that every customer has a salesperson to advise him or her while choosing jewelry?

   A. Sustainability

   B. Service

   C. Quality

   D. Cost competitiveness

   E. Innovation

Answer Key:

1. **(D) SPEED**—To succeed, managers must deliver performance. The fundamental success drivers of performance are innovation, quality, service, speed, cost competitiveness, and sustainability. Speed is rapid execution, response, and delivery.

2. **(B) COST COMPETITIVENESS**—Cost competitiveness means keeping costs low enough so that the company can realize profits and price its products (goods or services) at levels that are attractive to consumers.

3. **(B) SERVICE**—Service is the speed and dependability with which an organization delivers what customers want. An important dimension of service quality is making it easy and enjoyable for customers to experience a service or to buy and use products.

Day Five: Managing and Performing

 Improve Your Business Vocabulary

Key Marketing Terms

1. **Globalization:** the development of marketing strategies that treat the entire world (or its major regions) as a single entity

2. **Market Growth:** a stage of the product lifecycle when industry sales grow fast, but industry profits rise and then start falling

3. **Market Introduction:** a stage of the product lifecycle when sales are low as a new idea is first introduced to a market

4. **Market Maturity:** a stage of the product lifecycle when industry sales level off and competition gets tougher

5. **Product Life Cycle:** the stages a new-product idea goes through from beginning to end

6. **Sales Decline:** a stage of the product lifecycle when new products replace the old

Key Management Terms

1. **Innovation:** the introduction of new goods and services
2. **Quality:** the excellence of your product (good or service)
3. **Service:** the speed and dependability with which an organization delivers what customers want
4. **Speed:** fast and timely execution, response, and delivery

DAY SIX
Organizational Agility

"You can't add value to your clients until you find out what they value (...and value that)."

—Rashada Houston Turner, TruDream Enterprises

Day Six

Organizational Agility

In the prior section, we talked about how organizations survive and win over time by gaining and sustaining competitive advantages over competitors. We also discussed the role of innovation in developing those competitive advantages. Now, we'll discuss ways you can increase your advantage over the competition by improving the quality of your firm's goods and services. We'll develop these ideas from the perspective of **Total Quality Management (TQM)**, the philosophy that everyone in the organization is concerned about continuous improvement and quality to better serve customer needs.

How does TQM benefit the firm?. In business, success depends on having high-quality products. TQM is a comprehensive approach to improving product quality and thereby customer satisfaction. It is characterized by a strong orientation toward customers (external and internal). TQM reorients managers toward involving people across departments in improving all aspects of the business.

Most of the early attention in quality management focused on reducing factory product defects. At one time, most firms assumed defects were inevitable in mass production. They saw replacing defective parts or goods as just a cost of doing business—an insignificant one compared to the advantages of mass production. However, many firms were forced to rethink this assumption when Japanese producers of cars, electronics, and cameras showed that defects weren't inevitable. Much to the surprise of some product-oriented managers, the Japanese experience showed that it is less expensive to do something right the first time than paying to do it poorly and then pay again to fix the problems. Their success in taking customers away from established competitors made it clear that the cost of defects wasn't just the cost of replacement!

It is less expensive to do something right the first time than it is to pay to do it poorly and then pay again to fix the problems.

Firms that adopt TQM methods to reduce manufacturing defects can use the same approaches to overcome many other problems, such as poor customer service, flimsy packaging, or salespeople who can't answer customers' questions. From the customer's point of view, getting a defective product and having to complain about it is a big headache. In this case, the customer can't use the defective product and then suffers the inconvenience of waiting for someone to fix the problem. Instead of receiving superior value, the customer leaves dissatisfied, less trusting of the brand, and possibly spreading their disapproval to others via word-of-mouth, the Internet, and

> **The big cost of poor quality is the cost of lost customers.**

social media. The greatest cost of poor quality is the cost of lost customers.

Identifying customer needs and doing things right the first time seems obvious, but it's easier said than done. Problems always come up, and what isn't being done can be unclear. People tend to ignore problems that don't pose an immediate crisis. Nevertheless, firms that adopt TQM always look for ways to improve implementation with **continuous improvement**—a commitment to constantly make things better one step at a time.

As a business leader, you must deliver quality throughout the customer experience. Even one problem can affect how the customer perceives quality. The purchase and consumption process for many products involves multiple touchpoints. Think about how a rude waiter can ruin an otherwise great restaurant experience.

> **People tend to ignore problems that don't pose an immediate crisis. But firms that adopt TQM always look for ways to improve.**

Consider everything that needs to go right for a customer getting an oil change at a Firestone. The experience might begin at the Firestone website, where a customer seeks information about the service offered, prices, hours of operation, and the phone number and address of a local Firestone. Is this information easy to find? A friendly, knowledgeable person should promptly answer a phone call. Upon arrival, is the driveway well marked? Is there a long line for service? The attendant may have entered the license plate number and could already have the customer's details on the screen. Is the check-in process quick? Is the attendant courteous? The waiting area should be clean and perhaps offer Wi-Fi. What happens if another customer has noisy children? Does that affect the quality of the oil change experience? The payment process should be fast and offer information about the vehicle. The vehicle should be clean when it is picked up. Finally, the vehicle should not experience any service problems immediately following the oil change. Whew! That is a lot to get right every time if Firestone is to deliver high quality to its customers. Other types of products can have more or fewer touchpoints, but a business leader should recognize how they all contribute to the customer's perception of quality.

Extra Attention: Consider the points where there is contact between the customer and your company (i.e., touchpoints). Describe how you can improve customers' perceptions of quality at each touchpoint.

Touchpoint	Method to Improve Customer Perception of Quality
1.	1.
2.	2.
3.	3.
4.	4.
5.	5.

Day Six: Organizational Agility

 **Business Builder**

Source: Management: Leading & Collaborating in a Competitive World, By Bateman, T and Snell, S.

EXERCISE 6.1—UNDERSTANDING QUALITY

Objective

To examine how commitment to total quality requires a thorough, extensive, integrated approach

Instructions

Review Demming's "14 points" of quality below. Then consider how it can be used to develop an integrated approach to quality for your organization.

1. Create constancy of purpose
2. Adopt the new philosophy
3. Cease dependence on mass inspection
4. End the practice of awarding business based on price tag alone
5. Improve constantly the system of production and service
6. Institute training and retraining

7. Institute leadership
8. Drive out fear
9. Break down barriers among departments
10. Eliminate slogans, exhortations, and arbitrary targets
11. Eliminate numerical quotas
12. Remove barriers to pride in workmanship
13. Institute a vigorous program of education and retraining
14. Take action to accomplish the transformation

EXERCISE 6.2

Objective

To examine the importance of Six Sigma quality

Instructions

Review the definition of Six Sigma and the basis of The Malcolm Baldrige National Quality Award below. *Based on your understanding of quality and Six Sigma, how can your organization incorporate Six Sigma to increase customer satisfaction?*

1. **Six Sigma quality** is a method of systematically analyzing work processes to identify and eliminate virtually all causes of defects, standardizing the processes to reach the lowest practicable level of any cause of customer dissatisfaction

2. The Malcolm Baldrige National Quality Award encourages companies to achieve quality excellence, and is granted on the basis of seven criteria:

    A. Leadership

    B. Information and analysis

    C. Strategic quality planning

    D. Human resource development and management

    E. Management of process quality

    F. Quality and operational results

    G. Customer focus and satisfaction

EXERCISE 6.2—TEST YOUR KNOWLEDGE

1. Total quality management is a way of managing in which everyone is committed to the _____ of his or her part of the operation.

    A. fulfillment

    B. accountability

    C. concurrent engineering

    D. continuous improvement

    E. ethical standards

2. According to Deming's 14 points of quality, which of the following has to be eliminated, as they are contrary to the idea of continuous improvement?

    A. Numerical quotas

    B. Retraining programs

    C. Value chains

    D. Strategic alliances

    E. Just-in-time operations

Answer Key:

1. **(D) CONTINUOUS IMPROVEMENT**—Total quality management (TQM) is a way of managing in which everyone is committed to continuous improvement of his or her part of the operation. In business, success depends on having high-quality products.

2. **(A) NUMERICAL QUOTAS**—Deming's 14 points of quality emphasized a holistic approach to management that demands an intimate understanding of the process. One of the points is to eliminate numerical quotas since they are contrary to the idea of continuous improvement.

Day Six: Organizational Agility

 ## Improve Your Business Vocabulary

Key Marketing Terms

1. **Continuous Improvement:** a commitment to constantly make things better one step at a time
2. **Total Quality Management (TQM):** the philosophy that everyone in the organization is concerned about quality, throughout all of the firm's activities, to better serve customer needs

Key Management Terms

1. **Total Quality Management (TQM):** an integrative approach to management that supports the attainment of customer satisfaction through a wide variety of tools and techniques that result in high-quality goods and services
2. **Value Chain:** the sequence of activities that flow from raw materials to the delivery of a good or service, with the additional value created at each step

DAY SEVEN

External & Internal Environments: The Competitive Environment

Day Seven

External & Internal Environments: The Competitive Environment

The Competitive Environment

The **competitive environment** affects the number and types of competitors you will face and how you and the competition may behave. The competitive environment includes the companies with which your organization directly interacts. It also includes rivalries among current competitors and the impact of new entrants, substitute and complementary products, suppliers, and customers. Although you usually can't control the factors related to the competitive environment, you can choose strategies that avoid head-on competition. And where competition is inevitable, you can plan for it.

And where competition is inevitable, you can plan for it.

Economists describe four basic kinds of competitive market situations: pure competition, monopoly, monopolistic competition, and oligopoly.

Most product-makers lean toward **pure competition** or **oligopoly** over the long run. In these situations, competitors offer very similar marketing mixes. Recall from *Day Two* that the marketing mix consists of product, place, promotion, and price. Customers see alternatives as close substitutes when competitors fail to differentiate their offerings. In this situation, business leaders compete with lower prices and make less profit. Sometimes managers cut prices too quickly, without really thinking about how to add more customer value.

Business leaders can't just adopt the same "good" marketing strategies other firms use. That leads to head-on competition and a downward spiral in prices and profits. Business leaders must offer a marketing mix better suited to target customers' needs than the competition.

Monopoly situations in which one firm completely controls a broad product market, are rare. Further, governments commonly regulate monopolies. For example, in many parts of the world, prices set by utility companies must be approved by a government agency. While monopolies can be tempted to ignore customer needs, they often face competition sooner or later. Consider cable TV, which for a long time had a monopoly in delivering a wide range of television programming to homes. Cable TV operators were notorious for providing poor customer service. The competition came from satellite television and now from online providers like Hulu, Netflix, Amazon Firestick, and others. Many customers are happy to "cut the cord" because of memories of frustration with their cable television operator.

In **monopolistic competition,** several firms offer marketing mixes that at least some customers see as different. Each competitor tries to get control of its "own" target market. However, competition still exists because some customers see the various alternatives as a substitute. Most business leaders in developed economies face monopolistic competition.

In monopolistic competition, you would try to differentiate similar products by relying on other marketing mix elements. For example, many customers believe that most brands of gasoline are very similar. This makes it difficult for a Shell station to attract customers by claiming it offers better gas. So a Shell station might serve Seattle's Best Coffee, offer discounted car washes, maintain longer hours of operation, or keep a well-lit, safe storefront. Yet, such approaches may not work for long if competitors easily copy them. So business leaders should actively seek a **sustainable competitive advantage,** a marketing mix that customers see as better than a competitor's and cannot be quickly or easily copied by competitors.

The search for a breakthrough opportunity or some sort of competitive advantage requires an understanding not only of customers but also of competitors.

The best way to avoid head-on competition as a business is to find new or better ways to satisfy customers' needs and provide value. The search for a breakthrough opportunity or some sort of competitive advantage requires an understanding of customers and competitors. That's why marketing managers turn to **competitor analysis**—an organized approach for evaluating the strengths and weaknesses of current or potential competitor marketing strategies. A competitor analysis can help you identify potential opportunities and help you adapt the marketing mix to meet customer needs that are not being well-served by the competition.

You may recall from *Day One* that the basic approach to competitor analysis is simple. You compare the strengths and weaknesses of your current (or planned) target market and marketing mix with what competitors are doing or likely to do in response to your strategy. The initial step in competitor analysis is to identify potential competitors. It's useful to start broadly; from there it is easier to narrow down and target customers. Companies may offer different products to meet the same needs but become competitors when customers see them as offering close substitutes. **Competitive rivals** can be your closest competitors offering similar products. For example, Spotify competes with other streaming music services like Pandora, Songza, iHeartRadio, and Slacker, which provide similar services.

Companies may offer different products to meet the same needs, but they become competitors when customers see them as offering close substitutes.

Also, radio stations, software programs that organize music (Apple's iTunes), and music streaming services all compete as a broad set of competitors. This can help business leaders understand the different ways customers choose to meet their own needs and point to opportunities. For example, even music listeners who prefer a streaming service like Spotify must resort to radio stations or a playlsit while traveling in a car without a streaming connection. What customers choose and why can be valuable information for business leaders.

> **Extra Attention:** Identify companies that offer different products or services to meet the same need as your product or service. *Hint: If customers see them as offering close substitutes, then they are your rivals.*

_____

_____

_____

_____

_____

_____

_____

_____

You can use a **competitor matrix** to organize your competitive analysis. It compares the strengths and weaknesses of a company with those of its competitive rivals.

Extra Attention: Continue with the companies previously identified as offering close substitutes. Now, describe the strengths and weaknesses of these competitor rivals.

	Strengths	Weaknesses
Your Organization		
Competitor Rival #1		
Competitor Rival #2		
Competitor Rival #3		

As a business leader, you should actively seek information about current and potential competitors, although most firms try to keep the specifics of their plans secret. Public competitor information may be available. Sources include trade publications, sales reps, suppliers, and other industry experts. Customers may also be quick to explain what competing suppliers are offering.

The search for information about competitors can raise ethical issues. For example, people who change jobs and move to competing firms may have much information, but is it ethical for them to use it? Similarly, some firms have been criticized for going too far—like waiting at a landfill for competitors' trash to find copies of confidential company reports or "hacking" a competitor's computer network.

Beyond the moral issues, spying on a competitor to obtain trade secrets is illegal. The damages awarded for this behavior could be huge. For example, the courts ordered competing firms to pay Procter & Gamble about $125 million in damages for stealing secrets about its Duncan Hines soft cookies.

Competitors

When organizations compete for the same customers and try to win market share at the other's expense, all must react to and anticipate their competitors' actions.

The first question to consider is this: Who is the competition? Sometimes the answer is obvious. Walmart is one of the most successful brands in the retail business. It has retained the top position on the Fortune 500 list. What is the secret of the success of Walmart? What is Walmart's business strategy?

Walmart's mission statement is "to save people money so they can live better." Walmart's business strategies are a direct manifestation of this mission statement, and these strategies and purpose involve using price as a selling point to attract customers. Walmart fulfills the first part of its mission statement, "to save people money," by selling low priced goods through its stores compared to other mid-scale or high-end stores. Walmart's main competitive advantage is derived from its vision statement of selling low-cost goods.

As reflected in its mission statement, Walmart has successfully kept its products' prices low. This is also one of its greatest competitive advantages. There are various ways by which it has been able to do so, like keeping the cost of operations low, using the latest technology, establishing its distribution centers and warehouses at strategic locations, making its supply chain efficient through effective management, etc. Hence attracting customers by offering daily essentials at low prices is one of Walmart's main strategies.

Once competitors have been identified, the next step is to analyze how they compete. Competitors use price reductions, new product introductions, and advertising campaigns to gain advantages over their rivals. In its competition against PepsiCo, Coca-Cola outdoes its rival with much heavier spending on advertising. The emphasis on promotion helps the company win a larger share of not only the cola market but also juices (Coca-Cola's Minute Maid outsells PepsiCo's Tropicana) and sports drinks (Coca-Cola's Powerade is beating PepsiCo's Gatorade). PepsiCo has tried to catch up by spending more on advertising, but this gap is difficult to close.

Extra Attention: Continue with the companies identified as competitor rivals above. Assess their ability to compete with your organization.

	Your Organization	Competitor Rival #1	Competitor Rival #2
Your Organization	X		
Competitor Rival #1	X	X	
Competitor Rival #2	X	X	X

It's essential for you to understand what competitors are doing when you are honoring your strategy. If soft-drink consumption continues to fall, Coke must be careful not to be complacent about its leadership role versus Pepsi. Most of Coke's sales are beverages. Pepsi, in contrast, has expanded into a broader range of products, hoping to grow sales whether consumers are looking for a fun treat or a healthful snack. Besides reducing salt and sugar in traditional snacks such as chips, Pepsi is expanding to healthier options under its Quaker brand. These are areas in which Coke lacks a presence—but also are less profitable than soft drinks.

Competition is most intense when there are many direct competitors (including foreign contenders), when industry growth is slow, and when the product or service cannot be differentiated in some way. When an industry matures, and growth slows, profits drop. Then intense competition causes an industry shakeout; weaker companies are eliminated, and the strong companies survive.

Intense competition causes an industry shakeout; weaker companies are eliminated, and the strong companies survive.

New Entrants

New entrants into an industry compete with established companies. When many factors prevent new companies from entering the industry, the threat to established firms is less severe. On the flip side, if there are few barriers to entry, the threat of new entrants is more serious. Some significant barriers to entry are government policy, capital requirements, brand identification, cost disadvantages, and distribution channels.

Other barriers are less formal but can have some effect. Capital requirements may be so high that companies won't risk or try to raise such large amounts of money.

Brand identification forces new entrants to spend heavily to overcome established customer loyalty. Imagine, for example, the costs involved in launching a new cola against Coke or Pepsi. Established companies hold cost advantages due to large size, favorable locations, and existing assets, among other things.

Finally, existing competitors may have such tight distribution channels that new entrants have difficulty getting their goods or services to customers. For example, established food products already have supermarket or retail shelf space. New entrants are challenged to displace existing products with promotions, price breaks, intensive selling, and other tactics.

Substitutes and Complements

Besides products that directly compete, other products can affect a company's performance by being substitutes for or complements of the company's offering. A substitute is a potential threat; customers use it as an alternative, buying less of one product and more of another.

However, companies don't have to be at the mercy of customers switching to a substitute.

However, companies don't have to be at the mercy of customers switching to a substitute. To avoid losing out when others create new supplements, some companies try to create their supplementary products.

In response to a growing share of consumers caring about healthy snacking, Pepsi has invested in developing new sweeteners and healthier snacks to offer substitutes for consumers avoiding the calories, fat, and sugar.

Besides identifying and planning for substitutes, companies should also consider complements for their products. A complement is a potential opportunity because customers buy more of a given product if they also demand more of the complementary product. When people buy new homes, they also buy appliances and landscaping products. When they buy a car, they buy insurance for it. When buying a Kindle, they buy e-books, and when they buy an iPad, they buy various apps for playing games, reading the news, and many other activities. Similarly, when consumers munch on Lays, Doritos, or Cheetos snacks, they are bound to get thirsty and need a complementary product—say, an ice-cold Pepsi or Sierra Mist. PepsiCo owns all these food and drink brands; the company sells products that are complements and substitutes.

> **As with substitutes, a company needs to watch for new complements that can change the competitive landscape.**

As with substitutes, a company must watch for new complements that can change the competitive landscape.

Suppliers

Suppliers provide the resources needed for production, which may come in the form of people, raw materials, information, and financial capital. Suppliers are important to an organization for reasons beyond the resources they provide. Suppliers can raise their prices or provide poor-quality goods and services. Workers may produce either outstanding or defective work. Powerful suppliers can then reduce an organization's profits, especially if it cannot pass on price increases to its customers.

Organizations are disadvantaged if they become overly dependent on any powerful supplier. Of course, close supplier relationships can also be an advantage. For example, food and beverage companies work closely with the makers of the flavorings and additives that make their products appealing to consumers.

> **Organizations are at a disadvantage if they become overly dependent on any powerful supplier. Of course, close supplier relationships can also be an advantage.**

Increased competition requires managers to pay close attention to their costs. With the emergence of online shopping and social media, customers look for products built to their specific needs and preferences and want them delivered quickly at the lowest available price. This expectation requires the supply chain to be efficient and flexible so that the organization can quickly respond to changes in demand. Today, effective supply chain management aims to have the right product in the right quantity available at the right place at the right cost.

Choosing the right supplier is an important strategic decision. Suppliers can affect manufacturing time, product quality, and inventory levels.

Dr. Yvette Maureen

Customers

Customers purchase the goods or services an organization offers. Without customers, a company won't survive. Customers can be intermediate (wholesalers and retailers) or final (end users), depending on where they are in the value chain. When you buy a McDonald's hamburger or a pair of jeans from Macy's, you are a final customer. Intermediate consumers buy raw materials or wholesale products and then sell them to final consumers, as when Sony buys components from IBM and uses them to make Play Station consoles. Intermediate consumers make more purchases than individual final consumers do.

Like suppliers, customers are important to organizations for reasons other than the money they provide for goods and services. Customers can demand lower prices, higher quality, unique product specifications, or better service. They also can play competitors against one another, which occurs when a car buyer collects different offers and negotiates for the best price. Many companies are finding that today's customers want to be actively involved with their products, as when the buyer of an iPhone customizes it with ringtones, wallpaper, and various apps.

The Internet has further empowered customers. It provides an easy source of information—about product features and pricing. In addition, today's users informally create and share positive and negative messages online about a product. Companies try to use this to their advantage by creating opportunities for consumers and the brand to interact.

What is interactive marketing? Interactive marketing

is a tactic that uses engaging visuals or videos to get your audience to engage with your content. This form of marketing captures your audience's attention, delights them, and creatively presents your product or service. Online shopping is popular among many consumers. However, one of the downsides of online shopping is that customers aren't always able to try on a purchase before buying. Makeup company Lancome addresses this issue on its Instagram page by providing filters of different makeup shades users can access through their phone's cameras. This allows customers to see how a shade would look on their faces before deciding to buy. This is an example of augmented reality shopping. The feature allows visitors to Lancome's Instagram page or website to virtually "try on" some of the brand's products before purchasing, allowing them to purchase more confidently. The feature is easy to use; visitors can simply swipe through different shades the same way they would swipe through different filters on the app. Customer service means giving customers what they want or need, the way they want it, the first time. This usually depends on the speed and dependability with which an organization can deliver its products.

> **Customer service means giving customers what they want or need, the way they want it, the first time.**

Extra Attention: Where applicable, assign your organization a grade on the actions and attitudes below that demonstrate excellent customer service. Reflect on how you can earn straight A's.

Grade (A/B/C/F)	Excellent Customer Service Criterion (where applicable)
	Speed of filling and delivering normal orders.
	Willingness to meet emergency needs.
	Merchandise delivered in good condition.
	Readiness to take back defective goods and resupply quickly.
	Availability of installation and repair services and parts.
	Service charges (that is, whether services are free or priced separately).

You will operate with a disadvantage if you depend too heavily on powerful customers. Customers are powerful if they make large purchases or if they can easily find alternative places to buy. A firm's biggest customers have the greatest negotiating power, especially if they can buy from other sources.

Extra Attention: Think about who your organization's biggest customers are currently and in the future. Consider how you will leverage this position in future negotiations. *Hint: They may not be a current customer yet.*

_____

_____

_____

_____

_____

_____

DAY EIGHT

External & Internal Environments: The Economic, Legal, Political, Cultural, and Social Environments

Day Eight

External & Internal Environments: The Economic, Legal, Political, Cultural, and Social Environments

The Economic Environment

Economic conditions change over time and are difficult to predict. Bull and bear markets come and go. A recession may follow periods of dramatic growth. Every trend undoubtedly will end, but when? Even when times seem good, budget deficits or other considerations create concern about the future.

> **Every trend undoubtedly will end.**

Although most Americans think about the U.S. economy, the economic environment for organizations is much larger. The **economic environment** refers to macroeconomic factors (including national income, economic growth, and inflation) that affect consumer and business spending patterns. The rise and fall of the economy, in general, can greatly impact what customers buy.

The economic environment dramatically affects managers' ability to function effectively and influences their strategic choices. Interest and inflation rates affect the availability and cost of capital, growth opportunities, prices, costs, and consumer demand for products. Steeply rising energy and health care costs have significantly impacted companies' ability to hire and their cost of doing business. Unemployment rates affect labor availability, the wages the firm must pay, and product demand. During boom times, hiring accelerates, and unemployment rates fall. Generally, unemployment rises as workers are laid off in a recession (a period of falling economic output). Even a well-planned business strategy may fail if a country or region goes through a rapid business decline.

As a business leader, you must watch the economic environment carefully. In contrast to the cultural and social environment, the economic environment can move rapidly and require immediate strategy changes.

The Technological Environment

Today you simply cannot succeed as a business leader without incorporating the astonishing technologies that exist and continue to evolve into your strategy. Technological advances create new products and advanced production techniques, and create better ways of managing and communicating. In addition, as technology evolves, new industries, markets, and competitive niches develop. Technological advances also permit companies to enter markets that would otherwise be unavailable to them.

New technologies provide new production techniques. In manufacturing, sophisticated robots perform jobs without fatigue, requiring vacations or weekends off, or demanding wage increases. New technologies provide new ways to manage and communicate. For example,

» Computerized management information systems (MISs) make information available when needed, and networking via the Internet makes the information available where it is needed.

» Computers monitor productivity and note performance deficiencies.

» Telecommunications allow conferences to occur without requiring people to travel to the same location.

Such technological advances create innovations in business.

Most technological developments don't appear out of nowhere. Rapid advances in technology can shake up markets. Digital photography replaced film, which caused the bankruptcy of Eastman Kodak, once the world's largest film company. On the upside, the same digital technology created opportunities for new cameras from Nikon and Canon, and software

Rapid advances in technology can shake up markets.

from Apple (iPhone) and Adobe (Photoshop). Furthermore, the Internet opened up opportunities for breakthroughs, including Facebook, Twitter, and Instagram; new ways to deliver video entertainment, including YouTube and Hulu; and low-cost or free phone service from Skype or Vonage.

Consider the possible impact of Google's driverless car project. Many expect that most of us will be transported in robot-driven cars someday. There will be obvious effects in the automobile and insurance markets. Beyond that, did you know that auto accidents account for 2 million emergency room visits each year in the United States? So driverless cars may reduce hospital demand for emergency services. Also, the nation's elderly might be able to live on their own longer if they can get around without having to drive, slowing demand for nursing homes. Bars and restaurants may see more business and sell more alcohol when patrons don't need to worry about driving home under the influence. Business leaders who anticipate the impact of new technology can plan and adapt marketing strategies for the future.

New technologies give markets new ways to track consumers and perhaps deliver a more tailored experience, but does that invade consumers' privacy? Website visitors may not be aware that small computer files (called cookies) are often placed on their computers. Cookies allow the company to track what the customer does on the web. This information can be used to give a web surfer a better online experience, perhaps serving up useful information, advertising, and discounts. On the other hand, users are often tracked without their knowledge and may prefer to retain their privacy.

The Political Environment

The attitudes and reactions of people, social critics, and the government all affect the political environment. Consumers in the same country usually share a common political environment, and the political environment can also affect opportunities at a local or international level.

Strong sentiments of **nationalism,** an emphasis on a country's interest before everything else, affect how macro-marketing systems and business leaders work. For instance, The "Buy American" policy is included in many government contracts because there is broad consumer support for protecting U.S. producers and jobs from foreign competition. On the flip side, nationalistic feelings can reduce sales or block all marketing activities in some international markets.

The Legal Environment

Changes in the political environment often lead to changes in the legal environment, and, in a way, existing laws are enforced.

Businesses and individual managers are subjected to both criminal and civil laws. Penalties for breaking civil laws are limited to blocking or forcing certain actions, along with fines. Some of the most consequential business law issues are anticipated this year — from the potential overhaul of liability protections for third-party content online to the implosion of cryptocurrency firm FTX, to student loan debt relief. Big Tech companies, including Apple (AAPL), Amazon (AMZN), Google (GOOG), Meta (META), and Twitter, have new content, software, and transparency rules to abide by in the European Union. And companies of all sizes could see new rules in the U.S. for the user-generated content they host online. Beyond this, various laws regulate packaging and labels, telemarketing, credit practices, and environmental claims. Usually, the laws focus on specific types of products. The Food and Drug Administration (FDA) is an example of a regulatory body that can prevent a company from selling an unsafe or ineffective product to the public. It can seize products that violate its rules.

The Consumer Protection Safety Commission is a group with broad power to set safety standards and can impose penalties for failure to meet these standards. Given that the commission can force a product off the market—or require expensive recalls to correct problems—safety must be considered in product design. There is no more tragic example of this than the recalls of Firestone tires used as original equipment on Ford's Explorer SUV. Hundreds of consumers were killed or seriously injured in accidents.

The U.S. government's standards have restraints on business action regarding bribery. In some countries, bribes and kickbacks are common and expected ways of doing business, but for U.S. firms, they are illegal practices. Some U.S. businesses have been fined for using bribery when competing internationally.

In the end, laws can also assist organizations. Because U.S. federal and state governments protect property rights, including copyrights, trademarks, and patents, starting businesses in the United States may be more attractive than in countries where laws and law enforcement offer less protection.

Besides federal legislation—which affects interest commerce—business leaders must be aware of state and local laws. With the growth and continued norm of a hybrid and remote workforce, businesses face new challenges, including the need to adapt privacy policies and cybersecurity practices. These policies and practices should balance the needs of the business against employee and customer expectations regarding safeguarding personal information. No industry or business sector was safe in 2022 from cyberattacks. A glance at national and international headlines proved that: the Los Angeles Unified School District had a significant infrastructure disruption. An Australian telecom company suffered the largest cyber breach in history. Health insurers, educational institutions, and even an IT services consulting company – all hacked....
...Without a federal privacy law, states have looked to broaden the scope of data protection laws. With that, the marketplace has seen a flood of technology solutions designed to assist a business with its obligations. However, businesses need to be mindful that using these solutions might entail new privacy considerations, so confirming that the solution complies with the rules and regulations of your state and local jurisdictions is imperative.

The Cultural and Social Environments

Cultural and social environments have a broad impact on business. They affect how and why people live and behave as they do, which, in turn, affects customer buying behavior.

Many variables make up the cultural and social environment. Some examples are the languages people speak, the type of education they have, their religious beliefs, the type of food they eat, the style of clothing and housing they have, and how they view work, marriages, and family.

Over decades, the role of women has changed significantly. Sixty years ago, most people in the U.S. thought a woman's primary role was as a wife and mother in the home. More than 70 percent of women (aged 35 to 44) work outside the home. Such changes have increased household income, changed shopping habits, and generated a greater need for products, including childcare services and prepared take-out food. It has also changed who does the shopping for the household. Nowadays, almost half of all grocery shopping is done by men, and advertisers have been slow to craft ads that effectively speak to men.

> **Profitable markets require income as well as people. The amount of money people can spend affects the products they are likely to buy.**

Income is often one of the most important demographic dimensions when considering international markets. Profitable markets require income as well as people. The amount of money people can spend affects the products they are likely to buy. There are a variety of different measures of national income. One widely used measure is **Gross Domestic Product (GDP)**—the total market value of all goods and services provided in a country's economy in a year by both residents and non-residents of that country. **Gross National Income (GNI)** is a measure similar to GDP, but GNI does not include income earned by foreigners who own resources in that nation. By contrast, GDP does include foreign income.

When you compare countries with different international investment patterns, the income measures you use can make a difference. For example, Ford has a factory in Thailand. The GDP measures for Thailand would include profits from the factory because they were earned in that country. However, Ford is not a Thai firm, and most of its profits will ultimately flow out of Thailand. The Thai GNI would not include those profits. Using GDP income measures can give the impression that people in less developed countries have more income than they do. Further, in a country with a large population, the income of the whole nation must be spread among people. So, the GNI per capita (per person) is useful because it gives some idea of the income level of people in the country.

The more developed industrial nations—including the United States, Japan, and Germany—account for the biggest share of the world's GDP. In these countries, the GNI per capita is also quite high. This explains why so much trade occurs between these countries and why many firms see them as the most important markets. In general, markets like these offer the best potential for products that are targeted at consumers with higher income levels. Many managers, however, see great potential—and less competition—where GNI per capita is low.

A country's people's ability to read and write directly influences the development of its economy and business strategy planning. The degree of literacy affects how information is delivered, which in marketing means promotion. Illiteracy creates challenges for product labels, instructions, and print advertisements.

The adoption of technologies varies across the globe. Take cell phones, for example. Some people have separate phones for work and personal use, so the number of cell phones can exceed the population. Similar differences can be observed related to Internet access. You must be able to recognize how target markets utilize technology to determine their role in the business strategy. For example, setting up a whole website in another language may be more useful in some countries than others.

Another important dimension of U.S. society is its age distribution. While the U.S. population is not growing as quickly as in some other countries, the current population and population growth vary a lot in different regions of the U.S. The median age is growing because the percentage of the population in older age groups has increased.

Organizational Culture

One of the most important factors influencing an organization's response to its external environment is its culture. Organizational culture is the set of important assumptions about the organization and its goals and practices that members share. It is a system of shared values about what is important and beliefs about how the world works. In this way, a company's culture provides a framework that organizes and directs people's behavior on the job. An organization's culture may be difficult for an observer to define easily, yet like an individual's

The culture of an organization may be difficult for an observer to define easily, yet like an individual's personality, it can often be sensed almost immediately.

personality, it can often be sensed almost immediately. For example, how people dress and behave, how they interact with each other and with customers, and the qualities that are likely to be valued are usually quite different at a bank than at a law firm, and different again at an advertising agency.

For example, the Walt Disney Company's culture encourages extraordinary devotion to customer service; the culture at Apple Inc. encourages innovation. Employees in these companies don't need rulebooks to dictate how they act because these behaviors are conveyed as "the way we do things around here."

At Apple, the organizational culture is heavily centered around creativity and innovation. Company leaders have developed internal awards and programs that are designed to encourage employees to be creative in developing new products or solutions to company challenges. Because of their dedication to creativity and innovation, Apple has been able to remain on the cutting edge of technological advancement, which had led to a substantial base of brand-loyal customers.

A strong culture is consistent.

In contrast to strong cultures, weak cultures have the following characteristics: different people hold different values, there is confusion about corporate goals, and it is not clear from one day to the next what principles should guide decisions. Some managers may pay lip service to some aspects of the culture ("we would never cheat a customer") but behave very differently ("don't tell him about the flaw"). As you can guess, such a culture fosters confusion, conflict, and poor performance. Most business leaders would agree that they want to create a strong culture that encourages and supports goals and useful behaviors to make the company more effective.

Diagnosing Culture

A strong culture is consistent. The Ritz-Carlton hotel chain gives each employee a laminated card listing 12 service values. Each day it carries out a type of ceremony: 15-minute meetings during which employees from every department resolve problems and discuss areas of potential improvement. At these meetings, the focus is on the day's "wow story," detailing how a Ritz-Carlton employee lived up to one of the service values. In one instance, a family arrived at the Bali Ritz-Carlton with special eggs and milk because of their son's allergies, but the food had spoiled. The manager and dining staff couldn't find replacements in town, so the executive chef called his mother-in-law in Singapore and asked her to buy the necessary products and then fly with them to Bali, where the family was staying.

🔍 **Extra Attention:** Describe your company culture. List any areas of improvement. *Hint: Does everyone understand and believe in the firm's goals, priorities, and practice?*

_____

_____

_____

_____

_____

Managing Culture

Most companies today know that adopting a customer orientation and improving quality is necessary to remain competitive. As a top business leader, you can take several cultural management approaches. First, the vision—whether it concerns quality, integrity, innovation, or whatever—should be clearly articulated until it becomes a felt presence throughout the organization.

To reinforce the organization's culture, routinely celebrate and reward those who exemplify the new values.

Second, as an executive leader, you must pay constant attention to the daily affairs' mundane details such as communicating regularly, being visible and active throughout the company, and setting examples. Not only should you talk about the vision, but you should also embody it day in and day out. This increases credibility, creates a personal example others can emulate, and builds trust that the organization's progress toward the vision will continue over the long run. To reinforce the organization's culture, routinely celebrate and reward those who exemplify the new values.

Another key to managing culture involves hiring, socializing newcomers, and promoting employees based on the new corporate values. In this way, the new culture will begin to permeate the organization. As a result, the organization will be much more effective and responsive to its environmental challenges and opportunities.

Day Eight:
External and Internal Environments

 Business Builder

Source: Management: Leading & Collaborating in a Competitive World, By Bateman, T and Snell, S.

 EXERCISE 8.1—DISCUSSION QUESTION

Instructions

Consider the current business climate. Think about your answer to the following question. After reflecting on your response, read the prepared response below. *Hint: You can search online for help with your answer.*

Question

What changes do companies make in response to environmental uncertainty?

_____

_____

_____

_____

_____

Dr. Yvette Maureen

Answer:

Organizations may adapt to the environment by altering their work structures and work processes in order to reduce uncertainty. When uncertainty arises due to environmental complexity, many organizations adopt more decentralized decision-making structures that involve more parties and business units. This allows people with the most direct knowledge of a particular product or operation to make important decisions rather than a centralized unit that may be more removed from the daily business activities.

When uncertainty arises due to changes in the environment, many organizations adopt more flexible structures. When technologies, customers, and competitors change rapidly, a highly rigid, organization is less able to respond effectively, thus responsiveness and innovation become priorities.

Organizations can adapt to uncertainty by buffering at both the input and output sides of their boundaries. They may do this by hiring temporary workers during rush periods on the input side, and by maintaining adequate inventory in order to manage a rush of orders on the output side. Organizations may also adapt at their core by establishing flexible processes such as mass customization which allows an organization to produce large quantities at low cost, yet still offer individual customization.

Day Eight:
External and Internal Environments

 Improve Your Business Vocabulary

Key Marketing Terms

1. **Attitude:** a person's point of view toward something
2. **Belief:** a person's opinion about something
3. **Culture:** the whole set of beliefs, attitudes, and ways of doing things of a reasonably homogeneous set of people
4. **Drive:** a strong stimulus that encourages action to reduce a need
5. **Economic Needs:** needs concerned with making the best use of a consumer's time and money—as the consumer judges it
6. **Expectation:** an outcome or event that a person anticipates or looks forward to
7. **Needs:** the basic forces that motivate a person to do something
8. **Perception:** how we gather and interpret information from the world around us
9. **Personal Needs:** an individual's need for personal satisfaction unrelated to what others think or do

10. **Physiological Needs:** biological needs such as the need for food, drink, and rest
11. **Psychographics:** the analysis of a person's day-to-day pattern of living as expressed in that person's activities, interests, opinions—sometimes referred to as lifestyle analysis
12. **Safety Needs:** needs concerned with the protection and physical well-being
13. **Selective Perception:** people screen out or modify ideas, messages, and information that conflict previously learned attitudes and beliefs
14. **Selective Retention:** people remember only what they want to remember
15. **Social Needs:** needs concerned with love, friendship, status, and esteem—things that involve a person's interaction with others
16. **Trust:** the confidence a person has in the promises or actions of another person, brand, or company
17. **Wants:** needs that are learned during a person's life

Key Management Terms

1. **Maslow's Needs Hierarchy:** a conception of human needs into a hierarchy of five major parts
2. **Motivation:** forces that energize, direct and sustain a person's efforts

www.ingramcontent.com/pod-product-compliance
Lightning Source LLC
Chambersburg PA
CBHW052144110526
44591CB00012B/1850